NO-BAKE MAKES

Annalees Lim

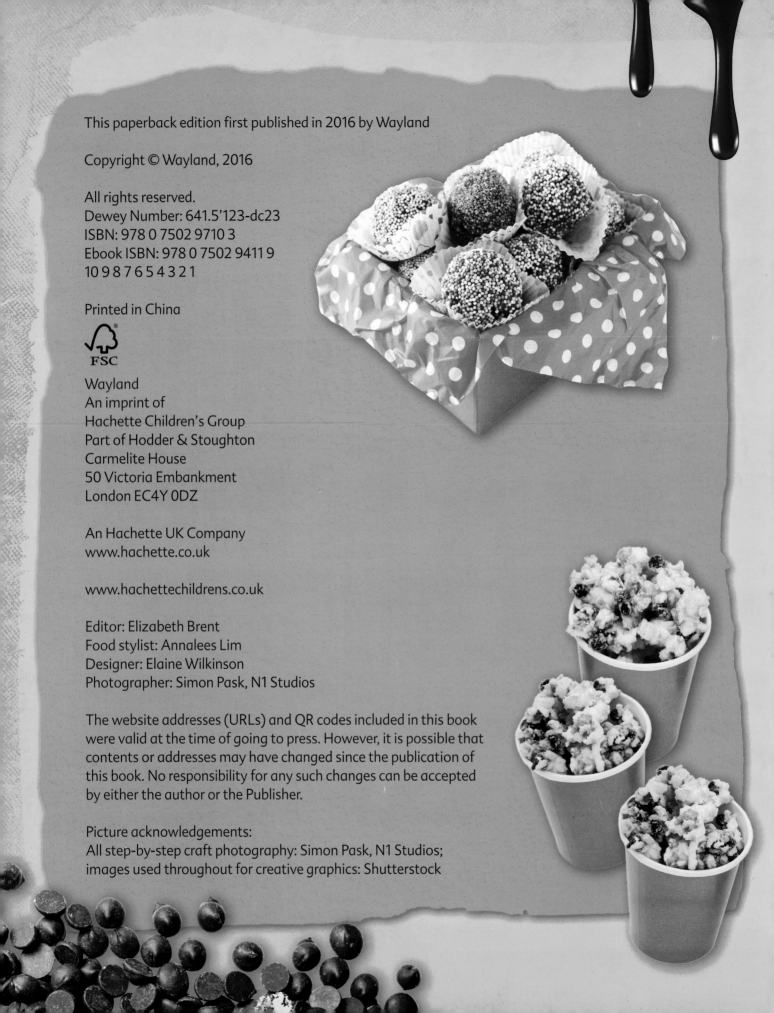

This paperback edition first published in 2016 by Wayland

Dewey Number: 641.5'123-dc23
ISBN: 978 0 7502 9710 3
Ebook ISBN: 978 0 7502 9411 9
10 9 8 7 6 5 4 3 2 1

Printed in China

FSC®

Wayland
An imprint of
Hachette Children's Group
Part of Hodder & Stoughton
Carmelite House
50 Victoria Embankment
London EC4Y 0DZ

An Hachette UK Company
www.hachette.co.uk

www.hachettechildrens.co.uk

Editor: Elizabeth Brent
Food stylist: Annalees Lim
Designer: Elaine Wilkinson
Photographer: Simon Pask, N1 Studios

Picture acknowledgements:
All step-by-step craft photography: Simon Pask, N1 Studios;
images used throughout for creative graphics: Shutterstock

Contents

No-bake makes 4

Strawberries and
cream cornflake cakes 6

Millionaires' biscuits 8

Lemon meringue bites 10

Penguin fruit fondue 12

Cake pop bites 14

Triple-choc iced biscuits 16

Peanut butter s'mores 18

Party popcorn 20

Rocky road 22

Glossary and Index 24

No-bake makes

Baking is a great way to make your own delicious cakes, biscuits and breads. This book is the perfect introduction to baking, and will show you fun and simple ways to make nine tasty treats without turning on an oven.

From delicious desserts to bite-sized biscuits, there is something here for anyone with a sweet tooth! If you are new to cooking, or just want to try something different, then this is a great first step into baking.

You won't need to use an oven, but for some recipes you will need to melt things, such as chocolate. You can ask an adult to help you use a microwave, or a bowl placed over a saucepan of hot water. Whichever method you use, always remember to take care when handling anything hot, and to make sure you don't let anything burn. You'll also need kitchen scales, to weigh out some of the ingredients.

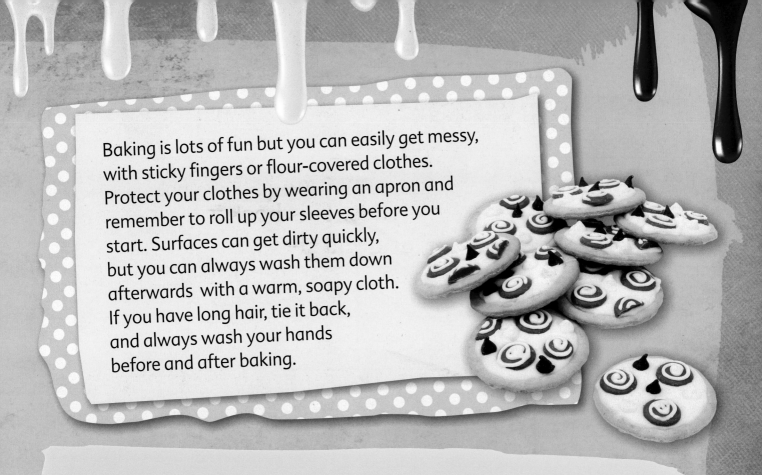

Baking is lots of fun but you can easily get messy, with sticky fingers or flour-covered clothes. Protect your clothes by wearing an apron and remember to roll up your sleeves before you start. Surfaces can get dirty quickly, but you can always wash them down afterwards with a warm, soapy cloth. If you have long hair, tie it back, and always wash your hands before and after baking.

This book is just the start of your baking adventure! You can experiment by changing ingredients to make up your own recipes. It's up to you how you cook and create your dishes; recipes are there to be changed, so do things your own way.

Baking for yourself is always a fun way to pass the time, especially if it is dull and rainy outside — but the best part is sharing what you have made and seeing how much other people enjoy it! So what's stopping you? Stock up your baking cupboard, put on an apron and choose your own no-bake make to create.

Strawberries and cream cornflake cakes

Makes 12

You will need:

- 250g white chocolate
- Vanilla extract
- 100g cornflakes
- 3 tablespoons dried strawberries
- 4 strawberry laces

- A 12-hole muffin tin
- 12 paper cake cases
- A large bowl
- A spoon
- A knife
- A chopping board or mat

These delicious cornflake cakes contain dried strawberries, making them perfect for a summer party!

1

Put the cake cases into the muffin tin.

2

Break the white chocolate into pieces in a large bowl, and melt it over a saucepan of hot water or using a microwave. Pour in a capful of vanilla extract and stir.

6

Mix in the cornflakes and dried strawberries, making sure everything is covered in chocolate.

Spoon the mixture into the cake cases.

Cut all four strawberry laces into three, and tie each part into a bow. Put a bow on top of every cornflake cake, then put them in the fridge to set.

Tip

Swap the berries for other dried fruit, such as cranberries (add orange extract instead of the vanilla extract), or cherries (add almond extract instead of vanilla to flavour).

Millionaires' biscuits

Makes 12

You will need:

- 25 digestive biscuits
- 75g butter
- 1 tablespoon golden syrup
- 1 tin (approx 400g) caramel
- 200g milk chocolate

- A square or rectangular dish
- Greaseproof paper
- Scissors
- A sandwich bag
- A wooden spoon
- A rolling pin
- A large bowl
- A metal spoon
- A small bowl

Millionaires' shortbread is always a favourite treat. Try making this version, using crushed digestive biscuits for the base.

1

Line the dish with greaseproof paper. Put the biscuits in the sandwich bag, and hit them gently with the back of the wooden spoon or a rolling pin to turn them into crumbs.

2

Melt 75g of butter in a large bowl, then tip in the crumbs and mix well.

3

Add the golden syrup to the crumb mix and then tip into the dish. Press down firmly with the back of a metal spoon.

4

Spread the caramel evenly over the biscuit base.

5

Melt the chocolate in a bowl, then pour it on top of the caramel. Put it in the fridge to set before cutting it into pieces.

Tip

If you gently shake the bag of biscuits, the larger pieces will rise to the top so you can easily see which bits still need to be made into crumbs.

Lemon meringue bites

Makes 6

T hese bite-sized meringues, filled with buttercream and lemon curd, make a delicious snack or gift.

You will need:

- 80g icing sugar
- 40g softened butter
- 12 mini meringues
- 3 teaspoons lemon curd
- 30g dark chocolate

- A small bowl
- A spoon
- A sandwich bag
- Scissors
- A chopping board or mat
- A wire cooling rack
- Greaseproof paper

1

Mix the icing sugar with the softened butter to make a stiff buttercream.

2

Put the mixture into the sandwich bag and cut off one corner. Pipe a swirl of buttercream onto six of the mini meringues.

3

Spoon half a teaspoon of lemon curd onto the six buttercream meringues.

4

Put the other six meringues on top of the lemon curd to make a sandwich. Place the meringue sandwiches onto a wire cooling rack, standing on top of some greaseproof paper.

5

Melt the dark chocolate and drizzle it over the meringue sandwiches. Leave until the chocolate has set.

Tip

Either soften your butter by keeping it out of the fridge or by putting it in a warm place like a windowsill or an airing cupboard. If you keep your butter in the fridge, then soften it slightly in a microwave before beginning.

Penguin fruit fondue

Makes 12

You will need:
- 12 grapes
- 60g dark chocolate
- White chocolate buttons
- orange and black icing pens

- 6 wooden skewers
- A small bowl
- A chopping board or mat
- A paper cup

Grapes, covered in chocolate and decorated to look like penguins, are the ideal party food. Your guests will want to eat a whole flock of them!

1

Wash your grapes and stick two on each skewer.

2

Melt the dark chocolate in a bowl and dunk each of the skewers into it. Make sure you completely cover the grapes.

Turn the paper cup upside down and pierce the bottom with the skewers so they stand up.

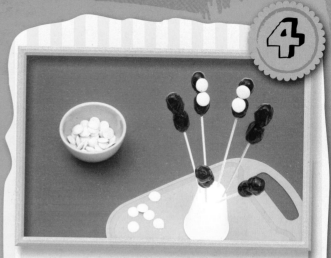

Press two chocolate buttons into the wet chocolate and put the penguins in the fridge to set.

Use the icing pens to draw on an orange beak and feet, and black eyes and wings.

Tip

Explore making other fruity creatures! Try making rabbits using a strawberry for the face and a chocolate button, cut in half, for the ears.

Cake pop bites

Makes 12

Cake crumbs and frosting, moulded into balls and covered in chocolate and sprinkles, make cake pop bites – delicious mini-treats that are perfect as presents.

1

Put the cake in a bowl, and break it into crumbs.

2

Add the frosting and mix well, using your hands. You want it to be the consistency of Play-Doh, so you may need to add more cake crumbs or frosting.

3

Mould the mixture into nine small balls of equal size.

4

Melt the chocolate in a bowl and drop each ball into it, making sure the ball is completely coated.

5

Drop each ball into the sprinkles or nuts and roll it around until it is covered. Repeat steps 4 and 5 for all of the balls, then put them in paper cake cases.

Tip

You could also try adding some fruit, white chocolate drops or popping candy to the mix!

Watch this step-by-step video of the cake pop bites being made!

Triple-choc iced biscuits

Makes 9

You will need:

- 75g icing sugar
- Water
- 9 plain biscuits
- Milk chocolate buttons
- Dark and white chocolate drops
- A white icing pen

- A small bowl
- A spoon
- A chopping board or mat
- A knife

Adding icing and chocolate buttons to plain biscuits transforms them into works of art!

1

Mix up some icing by adding small amounts of water to the icing sugar and stirring until smooth.

2

Cover each biscuit in a thin layer of icing, trying not to go over the sides.

3

Decorate the icing with chocolate buttons. You might want to cut some in half to make patterns.

4

Press chocolate drops in around the buttons.

5

Use the icing pen to decorate the buttons.

Tip

Try adding some food colouring to the icing to make multicoloured versions.

Watch this step-by-step video of the biscuits being decorated!

Peanut butter s'mores

Makes 6

You will need:

- Peanut butter
- 12 Plain biscuits
- 100g dark chocolate
- Mini marshmallows
- White chocolate chips

- A chopping board or mat
- A knife
- A small bowl
- A spoon

Eat one of these delicious marshmallow biscuit treats and you'll definitely want s'more! They are made up of layers of biscuit, peanut butter, chocolate and marshmallows.

Spread a thin layer of peanut butter on six of the biscuits.

Melt the dark chocolate.

3

Spoon a small amount of dark chocolate onto the peanut butter biscuits.

4

Scatter marshmallows and chocolate chips on top of the chocolate. Place the six plain biscuits on top of these.

5

Spread more chocolate on top of the biscuits and decorate with more marshmallows.

Tip

If you don't like peanut butter, you can make s'mores with jam, or even caramel.

Party popcorn

Party food doesn't get better than these crunchy popcorn slabs – mixed with chocolate, nuts and caramel sugar, they are ideal for snacking on!

1

Melt the white chocolate and mix it into the popcorn until it is all covered.

2

Add the golden syrup and mix well. The popcorn should be sticky, so you may need to add more syrup.

3

Mix in the chocolate drops, caramel sugar and chopped nuts.

4

Spread the popcorn in a layer on a sheet of greaseproof paper, and leave it to set.

5

Once it has set, break the popcorn up into chunks to serve.

Tip

You could also add dried fruit, popping candy, or even your favourite chocolate bar, chopped up into tiny bits!

Rocky road

Makes 12

You will need:

- 25 digestive biscuits
- 400g milk chocolate
- 50g butter
- 1 tablespoon marshmallows
- 1 tablespoon white chocolate chips
- 1 tablespoon dried cherries

- A large bowl
- A small bowl
- A spoon
- A cake tin
- Greaseproof paper
- A knife

This version of this versatile treat uses cherries, marshmallows and white chocolate, but you can add anything else you fancy!

1

Put the biscuits in a bowl, and crush them with the back of a spoon or your hands. You want a mixture of small chunks and larger pieces.

2

Melt 300g of the chocolate with the butter and mix it into the biscuits.

3

Add the marshmallows, chocolate chips and cherries to the mix.

4

Line the tin with the greaseproof paper and pour the mixture into it, pressing down well.

5

Melt the rest of the chocolate and cover the top of the cake in a thin layer. Leave to set before removing it from the tin and cutting into pieces.

Tip

You can use leftover cake, or other types of biscuit, to make the crumbs as the base for the rocky road. You can also add any other ingredients you like. Try raisins, or even some crystallised ginger pieces.

Glossary

airing cupboard a heated cupboard used for drying washing

fondue melted cheese or chocolate, for dipping pieces of food into

frosting cake icing

greaseproof paper special paper used in baking to line cake tins

pipe to use a bag with a nozzle to ice a cake or a meringue

s'more marshmallow and chocolate sandwiched between two biscuits

versatile easily adapted

Index

biscuits 8-9, 16-17, 18, 19, 23

cakes 6-7, 14-15, 23

chocolate 4, 6-7, 8-9, 12-13, 14-15, 16-17, 18-19, 20-21, 22-23

fondue 12-13
fruit 6-7, 12-13, 15, 21, 22

lemon curd 10, 11

marshmallows 18-19, 22-23

meringues 10-11

nuts 14, 15, 20-21

peanut butter 18-19
popcorn 20
popping candy 15, 21

rocky road 22-23
s'mores 18-19